Harriet Jacobs

Lydia R. Diamond

Inspired by
Incidents in the Life of a Slave Girl
by Harriet Jacobs

A SAMUEL FRENCH ACTING EDITION

SAMUELFRENCH.COM
SAMUELFRENCH-LONDON.CO.UK

Copyright © 2016 by Lydia R. Diamond
All Rights Reserved

HARRIET JACOBS is fully protected under the copyright laws of the United States of America, the British Commonwealth, including Canada, and all other countries of the Copyright Union. All rights, including professional and amateur stage productions, recitation, lecturing, public reading, motion picture, radio broadcasting, television and the rights of translation into foreign languages are strictly reserved.

ISBN 978-0-573-70435-2

www.SamuelFrench.com
www.SamuelFrench-London.co.uk

FOR PRODUCTION ENQUIRIES

UNITED STATES AND CANADA
Info@SamuelFrench.com
1-866-598-8449

UNITED KINGDOM AND EUROPE
Plays@SamuelFrench-London.co.uk
020-7255-4302

Each title is subject to availability from Samuel French, depending upon country of performance. Please be aware that *HARRIET JACOBS* may not be licensed by Samuel French in your territory. Professional and amateur producers should contact the nearest Samuel French office or licensing partner to verify availability.

CAUTION: Professional and amateur producers are hereby warned that *HARRIET JACOBS* is subject to a licensing fee. Publication of this play(s) does not imply availability for performance. Both amateurs and professionals considering a production are strongly advised to apply to Samuel French before starting rehearsals, advertising, or booking a theatre. A licensing fee must be paid whether the title(s) is presented for charity or gain and whether or not admission is charged. Professional/Stock licensing fees are quoted upon application to Samuel French.

No one shall make any changes in this title(s) for the purpose of production. No part of this book may be reproduced, stored in a retrieval system, or transmitted in any form, by any means, now known or yet to be invented, including mechanical, electronic, photocopying, recording, videotaping, or otherwise, without the prior written permission of the publisher. No one shall upload this title(s), or part of this title(s), to any social media websites.

For all enquiries regarding motion picture, television, and other media rights, please contact Samuel French.

MUSIC USE NOTE

Licensees are solely responsible for obtaining formal written permission from copyright owners to use copyrighted music in the performance of this play and are strongly cautioned to do so. If no such permission is obtained by the licensee, then the licensee must use only original music that the licensee owns and controls. Licensees are solely responsible and liable for all music clearances and shall indemnify the copyright owners of the play(s) and their licensing agent, Samuel French, against any costs, expenses, losses and liabilities arising from the use of music by licensees. Please contact the appropriate music licensing authority in your territory for the rights to any incidental music.

IMPORTANT BILLING AND CREDIT REQUIREMENTS

If you have obtained performance rights to this title, please refer to your licensing agreement for important billing and credit requirements.

HARRIET JACOBS was commissioned and given its world premiere by Steppenwolf Theatre Company (Martha Lavey, Artistic Director; David Hawkanson, Executive Director) in Chicago, Illinois on February 11, 2008. The performance was directed by Hallie Gordon, with sets by Collette Pollard, costumes by Ana Kuzmanic, lights by J.R. Lederle, sound by Victoria Delorio, original music by McKinley Johnson, choreography by Lisa Johnson-Willingham, and dramaturgy by Jocelyn Prince. The Stage Manager was Calyn P. Swain. The cast was as follows:

HARRIET JACOBS . . . . Nambi E. Kelly
GRANDMA . . . . Celeste Williams
MARY/ENSEMBLE FEMALE . . . . Leslie Ann Sheppard
TOM/ENSEMBLE MALE . . . . Christoph Horton Abiel
MAS. NORCOM/ ENSEMBLE . . . . Kenn E. Head
MS. NORCOM/ ENSEMBLE . . . . Genevieve Ven Johnson
SAMUEL TREADWELL SAWYER . . . . Sean Walton
JOSHUA/ENSEMBLE MALE . . . . Errón Jay

HARRIET JACOBS was first presented as a staged reading in May 2006 at the Kennedy Center, as part of New Visions/New Voices 2006.

HARRIET JACOBS was first performed in the United Kingdom on December 1, 2006 as a rehearsed reading at The Old Vic Theatre produced by Old Vic New Voices.

CHARACTERS
Note: All roles must be cast with black actors.

HARRIET JACOBS – (14-19) The author of the first published slave narrative. Harriet possesses an intelligence and centeredness beyond her years. These traits are equally attributable to the strength that surely any enslaved person must have had to endure, and a personal wisdom and acuity passed down from insightful parents and grandparents. Harriet has a social savviness, a dexterity that serves her well with her family, peers, and slave-owners. She's very educated, and slips easily between a more casual slave vernacular of the time to the formal language used in her writing, and when addressing the audience. She is not "putting this on" or "talking proper"; she is an adept and unconscious "code-switcher." Historically Harriet is described as having light brown skin and dark eyes. She is the daughter of two bi-racial parents. She is pretty, but does not embrace nor consciously exploit her looks. In her setting, they are more often a liability than a blessing and she is aware of this.

GRANDMA – Well-liked, free grandmother.

ENSEMBLE (FEMALE):

> **MARY** – African American. 15. In awe of and dangerously jealous of Harriet. A house servant and field hand, and has fewer of Harriet's social and language graces.
>
> **CHARLOTTE**
>
> Various other roles.

ENSEMBLE (MALE):

> **TOM** – African American, 18. Handsome, strong, good natured, charismatic. He loves Harriet.
>
> **HAROLD**
>
> Various other roles.

ENSEMBLE (MALE) / MAS. NORCOM – 50-65. The White Master. The town doctor, he carries himself with a confident swagger. He fancies himself a Godly, family man. (Avoid casting him as the obvious villain.) Various other roles.

ENSEMBLE (FEMALE) / MS. NORCOM – The White Mistress. 27. A faded flower. Once beautiful and carefree, she is a victim of her environment. She is hateful toward her female slaves and wary of her husband. She has born a child a year since her marriage at 17. Various other roles.

SAMUEL TREADWELL SAWYER –White Lawyer. 30s. From a prestigious family. He is intrigued by Harriet's intellect, and physically attracted to her. He is probably not "in love" with her.

ENSEMBLE (MALE) / JOSHUA – 61. A strong-willed field hand and various other roles.

CHILDREN – Harriet's children – Preferably children but could be played by adult ensemble. They are not necessarily required to speak.

A Quick Note from the Playwright.

So, there's something I wish to tell you. Something I've learned while continually revising through many early rehearsal processes, workshops, and sessions with brilliant dramaturgs, friends, and colleagues.

Every time I enter a new rehearsal process I am taken by how incredibly emotionally challenging it is to inhabit the people, feelings and customs of this obscene institution (slavery). This is what theatre artists do, and while we're absolutely up to the task, because we have been trained to do our homework, be open, be present, be vulnerable, sensitive, and precise, it can still be daunting.

Through the writing of this piece, I have felt sometimes so utterly inadequate. How do I presume to honor this reality that my ancestors lived? How can I, a consumer of so many infantilized, exoticized, romanticized, sanitized images of slavery, do justice to the portion of Harriet Jacobs' remarkable life that I wish to share with you?

And this is what I have learned. I am obligated to try. I'm a playwright and when there is a story to tell, I am compelled to tell it. I want Harriet Jacobs to exist, theatrically, alongside Anne Frank and Joan of Arc, because she deserves to. Because young and old, we need her.

This is also what I have learned. It is hard not to drown in the presumed misery of it all, before cracking the book open, before the house lights even come down.

When you read this play, act this play, direct or produce this play, try not to dwell only in the pain of it. Try, I think, to humbly acknowledge that we bring to it what we do, through the perspectives that we have, whether you agree that it is a slightly skewed perspective or not, and then put that aside and live in the present I've tried to create.

In her book, *Incidents in the Life of a Slave Girl*, Ms. Jacobs works to articulate to us the horrors of slavery. In my play, I work to articulate the psychological conundrum of trying to put words to that which is unspeakable. I work to celebrate the humanity that lived between and around the pain. That my ancestors who were enslaved people, lived and cried, and loved and laughed, agitated and manipulated, more fully aware of their own predicament than we'll ever be, but always human and always with a will to live.

Honor, please, the humor in this play, where there is humor. Honor the burgeoning affections where they exist. The familial love where it lives. Try not to plod through it with a guilty, pained, apologetic, pitying, angry, contemporary sensibility – that's too easy. Let it live please, from moment to moment, from laughs to tears, as we live life, walking through the murk of our personal and societal contradictions. We owe it to Ms. Jacobs. We owe it to the ancestors.

ACT I

Scene One

(A light reveals a crude wooden shed, about eight feet high. The shed has only the suggestion of walls and a roughly hewn slanted roof, it is only slightly larger than the space under a conference room table.)

*(**TWO MALE CAST MEMBERS** unlatch the sides of the structure's roof, to reveal **HARRIET**, lying on her stomach, writing by candlelight in the small space, now indicated by a skeletal frame.)*

(The candle goes out. Blackness.)

HARRIET. It is a dark that is darker than light. *(**HARRIET** strikes a match, lights candle, writes furiously, candle blows out. Darkness.)* Blacker even than that. *(**HARRIET** lights candle again, resumes writing. After a moment she notices audience.)* Today black and small and damp and cold. Tomorrow maybe hot and dry. Full of splinters that bite, and mites that bite, and vermin that bite. Are you there? I am never sure. I see faces in my darkness... until I am alone, again.

> *(**HARRIET** climbs down the ladder, and crosses to center.)*

I must explain. *(**HARRIET** rolls up her sleeve.)* If you would understand. Please. I try to understand myself. This reality that has brought me to, this reality. I try to make sense of it, and so I ask that you try as well. I fear that if I say to you that what I experienced under the cruel hand of slavery was unspeakable… I fear that you would incline your heads a bit to the left or the right and say, "Yes, I understand, poor girl," and think no more of it. I fear more that you might throw your head back in exasperation and say, "Tell us something we have not already heard." I promise, I shall try. We shall all try.

> *(Music begins. Voices of the ensemble begin humming an a cappella spiritual. [Spirituals should be appropiate to the 1800s.])*

I promise that you may believe you have heard it, you may believe you know this, and I suggest that it is slightly beyond knowing, because still, I hear the stories, I live the stories and I do not yet understand. *(beat)* This is the flesh. My flesh. My feet. My head. My heart. It is all I have to offer. It is all we have to offer.

> *(**MALE ENSEMBLE** members emerge from the shadows, transforming the austere stage into **GRANDMOTHER**'s kitchen.)*

I have misspoken. Not ours. Not my flesh. Not my body. Even now, not mine. *(touching her body) (beat)* My *soul.* This is mine. This has always been mine. My heart, my soul, this is what I wish to share. With you.

> *(Light rises on an old lady, kneading bread on a small table by a hearth. **HARRIET**'s **GRANDMOTHER**…)*

GRANDMA. Who are you talkin' to?

HARRIET. To whom am I talking Grandma…

GRANDMA. I am sure my granddaughter is not tellin' *me* how to speak…

HARRIET. I'm jes teasing with you.

GRANDMA. *(laughing)* Better be… 'cause seems to me, I'm the one taught you, in your diapers, to say your first words…so, who were you talkin' to? …

HARRIET. Oh, I was just…just thinking.

GRANDMA. Well stop that. Life *is*. We pray to the Lord for deliverance, love the people before us whom we must love, wipe our butts, roll up our sleeves and work. No time for thinking.

HARRIET. *(laughing)* Wipe our butts? What's gotten into you?

GRANDMA. Little bit of the devil today I s'pose. Did I add the leavening?

HARRIET. Probably.

GRANDMA. Take that batch out, they smell ready.

(**HARRIET** *moves to look out of the window.*)

HARRIET. It's getting late…

GRANDMA. They burning…

HARRIET. *(removing the crackers)* She'll have my hide.

GRANDMA. So take the Mistress a package of warm crackers. Tell her Grandmother wouldn't let you leave 'fore they come out. How many babies she drop, one a year fo de lass six years? Tell her maybe if she cross her legs and eat a cracker, wouldn't be in that condition all the time.

(**HARRIET**'s *removing crackers from a cookie sheet as they speak.*)

HARRIET. If it's just the same to you, I think I won't tell her the latter.

GRANDMA. The latter? You need to watch it with the fancy talk.

HARRIET. I speak from my heart, and so, if my heart is smarter than my master's I cannot help it, and I will not apologize for it.

GRANDMA. Just tell me this. How he have time to run after skirt like he do…? Got her always in the family way, seem he gettin' enough where he lay.

HARRIET. Grandmother stop…

GRANDMA. That's why she so mean, can't lay down for rest for he tryin' to climb on top of her…

HARRIET. Grandmother…

GRANDMA. And if she do lay down, cain't rest proper tryin' to figure out who else he climbin' on top of. Should jes be grateful for a moment of peace on her back...

(Both laugh.)

*(The door opens and two "**WHITE* LADIES**" enter. **GRANDMOTHER** and **HARRIET**'s postures change to proud deference, no hint of the mirth from the moment before. *Note: All "white" characters are represented by **BLACK ENSEMBLE** members, donning skeletal white hoop skirts, bonnets, top hats, white gloves, or the like.)*

WHITE LADY 1 (MARY). Molly, I need cornbread for a stuffing...

GRANDMA. *(pointedly)* Good evening to you, Ma'am.

WHITE LADY 1. Yes, of course... Good evening. *(before **GRANDMOTHER** can respond)* I need cornbread, the older and harder the better...

GRANDMA. Well ma'am, I jes' gave the pigs the day olds, but if you slice the new down the middle and toast it, it should serve your dressing just fine.

WHITE LADY 2. I hope you have a pass Harriet.

GRANDMA. May I offer your order as a gift, an' in exchange you drop Harriet off at the back of the Norcom estate, splainin' to the Mistress how you ran 'cross her here and asked her to help carry your load.

WHITE LADY 1. Then you will need to add a dozen vanilla wafers to the order.

GRANDMA. Yes ma'am.

WHITE LADY 1. And a couple of those petit fours.

GRANDMA. Yes ma'am.

WHITE LADY 2. Oh, well, I'll have a dozen wafers as well.

GRANDMA. Certainly. *(beat)* That'll be twelve cents.

WHITE LADY 2. Oh…

> *(She turns to* **LADY 1**, *who shrugs.)*

Oh…

> *(She looks in her purse.)*

Maybe just a half dozen then.

> *(She pays.)*

GRANDMA. Harriet, get your shawl.

HARRIET. Thank you grandmother. I see you soon I hope.

GRANDMA. I love you baby. *(pulling her aside)* Please try not to let that mouth get you in trouble.

Scene Two

> (**HARRIET** *enters, carrying a heavy bucket of water and ladle on her head. A rhythmic, muffled work song is heard under the scene...* **HARRIET** *sets down the bucket, removes a small book from her pocket and begins to read.* **TOM** *walks up to her...* **HARRIET** *is startled...quickly putting the book the in her pocket.*)

HARRIET. Lord! Tom! You near scared the devil out of me...

TOM. Harriet?

HARRIET. What you doin'?

TOM. Came to see you. I see what you doin'. You need to be more careful.

HARRIET. Had a moment, thought the workers could use a bit of water. An' they wasn't here, an' I was at a real good place in the story...

> *(Beat. They stand and grin at one another.)*

Tom.

TOM. Uh huh...

HARRIET. Naw, I ain't got nothin' to say, I jes like the way it sounds... Tom. I like the way it taste, your name in my mouth.

TOM. Seems like the name Ezekial, or Elijah might taste better in your mouth.

HARRIET. Maybe would, but I fancy Tom. *(beat – teasing)* If you think it best, I might could go lookin' for a 'Zekial or a 'Lijah to spend my time with.

TOM. Brought somethin' to show you.

> (**TOM** *pulls an ornate piece of a banister out of his bag.*)

HARRIET. It's beautiful. *(beat)* What is it?

TOM. It's the part what holds up a banister. See how sturdy but handsome to look at? I made a tool that makes it easy to do with just one piece of wood. It's a trick in it, an' I figured out how, an' I think it's gone set me up real nice. In jes' a few minutes all Master's cronies gone be asking to hire me out to give them somethin' so fancy.

HARRIET. It's clever. You think you get your own shop one day?

TOM. May, or maybe I jes be a carpenter for hire. Make a living, support a family someday.

> (**HARRIET** *smiles shyly, doesn't allow the tone to change to serious as* **TOM** *would have it.*)

HARRIET. *(putting her hands behind her back)* Guess which one...

TOM. I don' have time for playin games...

HARRIET. Jes guess.

> (**TOM** *points to a hand.* **HARRIET** *opens it and a ball of cotton falls out.*)

Good. Try again.

> (**HARRIET**, *picks up cotton, puts her hands behind her back, and presents her fists again.*)

Twice. You get three right, I give you a kiss.

TOM. You silly.

> (*And again she puts her fists out.*)

HARRIET. Awright then.

> (**TOM** *guesses right a third time.* **HARRIET** *kisses him, quickly on the mouth.* **TOM** *starts to leave.*)

Wait Tom. Can you keep this for me, so we can play next time I see you, even if it's not in the cotton field.

> (**TOM** *crosses back.* **HARRIET** *hands him a cotton ball.*)

Wait.

> (*And the other from the other fist. They both laugh heartily.*)

TOM. You bad.

HARRIET. Yes I am. I most certainly am dear Tom.

*(As **TOM** exits, the work song becomes stronger, until **HARRIET** is surrounded by workers…the work is shown in synchronized, highly choreographed, rhythmic movement. Eventually, each worker drops his or her song to sip from the kettle and sit under a tree. When the last worker has taken a sip, and the bucket with him, the song has finally dwindled.)*

HARRIET. *(to house)* If you have not seen a cotton field, when the cotton is almost ready for picking, you have missed one of the most beautiful sights God has given us. I like to kneel in the middle of an' open field, so the cotton is just below my eyes. For as far as you can see it looks like a soft blanket, or maybe even heaven. I think God has given the south cotton because he does not often give us snow.

(Song begins, continues under:)

Sometimes I lie on my back and look at the clouds and I feel as though I just might melt on up into them. I close my eyes an' try not to think…

HAROLD (ENSEMBLE). Name's Harold. Work de fields. Forty-sebben years ole. Live here all my life. Blessed by God 'cause I never got solt away from my fambly.

HARRIET. …I am sorry for you if you have not seen a cotton field, when the cotton is almost ready for picking.

HAROLD. Only time I remember a real beatin', was day 'fore my eighteenth birfday. Took a liken' to a young girl worked next ta me in de fields.

HARRIET. Juss soff an white an' little specs of brown…

Is so soff…

HAROLD. Overseer caught us spendin' time together 'hind a tree on break. She was a good girl.

HARRIET. It truly is breathtaking. It is the one time when I feel most unburdened.

HAROLD. Weren't doin' nothing put her in a way bring shame to her or her fambly.

HARRIET. ...As though my heart would float up an be one with the blue sky above me, and my body would just follow along.

HAROLD. So, dis overseer calls all de workers over...

HARRIET. Like I be light as a feather, maybe shifting this way and that, depending on the strength of the wind.

HAROLD. Make them stand all around us in a circle...

HARRIET. I close my eyes an' try to close my ears an' heart to the stories...

(*HARRIET lies down...*)

HAROLD. Overseer make us get undress an tell us to do things we wouldna even done by ourselves.

HARRIET. The clouds real pretty...

HAROLD. Her mama, two aunts, an' a grandpappy had to watch me lay on top of her. An' jes then I think, don' matter what happen to me, 'cause de lord don' wan' people ackin like dis.

HARRIET. And the blue of the sky bluer than any blue...

HAROLD. An I get offa her an ah put on my pants an ah tell Overseer he gone have to finish what I start 'cause I too young to go ta hell fo his sins. An he beat me so hard I couldn't lay down t'sleep fo the pain. Only part my body not scarred to dis day from dat beatin's de bottom my feet.

HARRIET. Maybe the sky not that blue...

HAROLD. De girl, don't know what had happen' to her.

(*Silence. A shift.*)

HARRIET. I see the blood and sweat and tears dripping off my pretty cotton and it not so pretty. (*beat*) My work is elsewhere. Easier because I do it with a roof over my head, shoes on my feet, and the North Carolina sun off my back.

(HARRIET steps downstage and speaks to audience so fieldhands can't hear)

HARRIET. Harder maybe 'cause I see life on the other side of misery. Harder 'cause I live under the feet of the whites who wish us to believe that we are animals.

(The light shifts, and we are inside. Bags that had been slung over arms for picking, and bundles that represented babies on backs, reveal a small chandelier, candles, aprons the women don, vests the men put on, furniture, etc. It is all hustle and bustle, as the field hands become house servants.)

HARRIET. It is quite amazing really, the inner workings of the "big house."

(rhythmic, fast tempo, work music)

I don't think Mistress Norcom would know how to keep it going were it not for the administrative skills of the head male servant, the female cook, and the various household talents of the rest of us.

*(The "house" is set up as **HARRIET** speaks. This is both a highly choreographed depiction of **HARRIET**'s work day, and a portrayal of the cat and mouse game that goes on between **HARRIET** and the **MASTER**. The whole **ENSEMBLE** is involved.)*

First thing in the morning, before the sun comes up, I empty the bedpans.

*(**MASTER NORCOM** hands **HARRIET** a bedpan, catches her wrist and whispers into her ear.)*

I then rekindle the fires in each and every room. I help the mistress with her morning toilette…

*(A "servant" transforms into the **MISTRESS**, with Harriet's assistance as she talks. **MASTER NORCOM** lurks but does not approach **HARRIET**.)*

This includes the second removal of a bedpan, heating and carrying water for a bath, the combing and arranging of hair, stockings, petticoats, and skirts, and the fastening of each and every button.

> *(As* **HARRIET** *leaves the* **MISTRESS**, **MASTER NORCOM** *catches the* **MISTRESS** *by her wrist, whispers in her ear and pats her bottom, she exits,* **MASTER** *walks to* **HARRIET** *and whispers in her ear.)*

Once the house is awake I hang the rugs on the line out back and beat them. I wash and polish the floors.

> *(***MASTER NORCOM*** admires her in her knelt position.)*

I clear and wash breakfast dishes. I dust each baseboard. I wash the windows. I polish the silver.

> *(***MASTER NORCOM*** whispers in her ear.)*

I clear and wash the lunch dishes. I mend clothes, darn socks, and iron linens. I lay the rugs back down.

> *(***MASTER NORCOM*** whispers.)*

and on and on it goes. And this is my reality. But worse than mine, today...are the stories that never stop...

> *(The hustle and bustle, the rhythms and movement of work continue at top speed. A very old* **CHARLOTTE NORCOM [ENSEMBLE]** *steps forward, struggling with a basket of laundry. The work continues behind her.)*

CHARLOTTE. I born here. People 'member de ole master an missus as decent an' good 'cause dey went to church, hab a big, well dressed fambly, an kep' all us slaves clean an fed. Dat massa, de doctor's daddy, was always after me, had me too, 'cause I was der and dats what dey could do. Missus din' like it. She always steady lookin' at me like I her worsest enmy. Affer my third baby come out lookin' mo like de massa din de massa hisself, she come to my cabin, night affer de birf an takes him. Don' know if she kilt de baby or solt him. I think probly kilt him 'cause none de house servants never could look me in de eyes affer dat. Still, dey kep me on, an one day she jes start ta beatin me wiff a iron kettle rod. She sho woulda beat me to my deaf, loss my leff eye dat day, but de rod broke an she had to stop long 'nuff to hear me say, "God fo sho cryin fo you today." I say, "I sho wouldn't treat a dog as you treatin' me." An she stop an commence to fall on de flo' cryin', an I comfort her. Later I get a whippin' 'cause some blood dripped on the Mistress's silk skirts. Dey long dead now.

> (**CHARLOTTE** *recedes into the working* **ENSEMBLE**. *Their efforts dwindle and they exit, as* **HARRIET** *steps forward.*)

HARRIET. The only real escape is the time I spend in the loving cocoon of Grandmother's kitchen, with the two people I love most in the world. It is not just the sweet smell of cinnamon rolls mingled with the sharp scents of sage and parsley…it is the warm embrace of unconditional love. The comfort of my steady Tom and Grandma's incomparable sass…

> (*As* **HARRIET** *speaks she moves into* **GRANDMA**'s *kitchen where* **GRANDMA** *and* **TOM** *sit eating biscuits and gravy.*)

GRANDMA. Incomparable sass…there you go again with the words.

TOM. We love your words Harriet… But, I still tryin' to see whatchu gettin' at?

HARRIET. Jess that I believe there are two kinds of mean Mistresses.

TOM. It don't matter.

HARRIET. Hear me Tom… There are Mistresses who know that this *(beat)* …

GRANDMA. What?

HARRIET. How it is…this way we live… Slavery…

GRANDMA. Lord have mercy…can't you never talk 'bout who was seen goin' into the tool shed with who…like a normal girl. An I don't like to gossip, but it was Annie an' that boy what works in the house, they call him Red...

HARRIET. Still, I am making a point. There are those mistresses who know that this thing, this way we live, slavery, is evil and wrong and so lash out because they must convince themselves that we are animals that they might sleep at night, and hold their heads up in church on Sunday morning.

GRANDMA. *(offering* **TOM** *another biscuit)* Another biscuit Tom?

TOM. Please. Thank you ma'am.

GRANDMA. I jes noticed 'cause I think Red at least five years younger than that girl. An whatever they was doin' in the tool shed, they didn't come out the shed with not even a hammer...

HARRIET. It is as though I am not talking.

TOM. It is never as though you are not talking.

HARRIET. And then there are those Mistresses who would treat their own meanly, and so certainly would have no regard for us. An' all of them, steady getting treated mean by they own men.

TOM. And God sees only the mean behavior, and would not care why.

HARRIET. If I can distinguish between the two, certainly God can.

GRANDMA. Because you sit on the right hand of God the father almighty?

HARRIET. Because I have the thought, and the thought must be put there by God.

TOM. Now you sound like the Master. "God has told me that I must take care of you black heathens because you cannot see after yourselves."

HARRIET. I just think that the Mistress who only beats me because she is miserable, hurts when she does, and so will be judged accordingly.

GRANDMA. And so you believe you'll sit at the table of milk and honey next to the woman who beat you?

HARRIET. Oh no Granny, she'll be servin' me at the table.

TOM. *(laughing)* See this is what brings me 'round even when I may pay for it tomorrow.

GRANDMA. I thought it was my biscuits.

TOM. You thought wrong old lady.

HARRIET. Tom!

GRANDMA. *(laughing)* He's right, start thinkin' too much of yourself when folks all time tellin' you 'bout your talents.

TOM. Those talents bought your freedom, so you keep right on thinkin' highly of them.

GRANDMA. But long as he owns my kin, I am still under the thumb of the good Doctor Norcom.

HARRIET. He can't touch you, he wouldn't dare. Don't want the town to see his true colors.

TOM. Truth be told, it is your beauty, not your biscuits brings me round.

HARRIET. What about my beauty?

GRANDMA. Don' worry, I ain' gone steal yo man.

TOM. I think you should worry Harriet. Grandma lookin' good today…

GRANDMA. I'm goin' to the shed, be back in four minutes.

> (**GRANDMA** *exits to shed.* **HARRIET** *moves to* **TOM**'s *lap.*)

TOM. You noticed she always tellin' us jes' how long. "I be back in three an' a half minutes, an' forty seconds."

HARRIET. But it's never long enough for me to get a good kiss.

> *(They kiss.)*

TOM. I thought that was pretty good.

HARRIET. But not long enough.

> *(They kiss again.)*

TOM. Long enough for me to get worked up though.

HARRIET. She wants you worked up, so you'll ask for my hand.

TOM. I woulda done that a long time ago if I thought it was yours to give.

HARRIET. So you would deprive me the joy of hearing you ask?

TOM. To spare myself the pain of having him say no. Or worse, he convince my master to sell me away.

HARRIET. Or sell me away.

TOM. He ain't thinkin' 'bout sellin you away. Not how he be all the time lookin' at you.

HARRIET. Doesn't that bother you?

TOM. I lose my mind, I be bothered by that. He is still just lookin' at you?

HARRIET. Yes, but don't say nothin' to Grandma 'bout it, please. She worry too much, may even say somethin' cross to him and get me sold down the river. *(beat)* Tom, you think we can run from this one day?

TOM. We ain' gone have to run. We gone buy our freedom.

HARRIET. Don' you think we gone make some pretty, smart babies Tom?

TOM. Don' know I wan' bring babies into dis kind of a world.

HARRIET. Don' think there's nothin' you can do 'bout that. Not if you love me like you says you do. 'Sides ain' gone make no babies jes kissen' fo four minutes…

TOM. I can wait Harriet…we say the words, jump de broom and then make the babies… We ain't got to live like animals, jes 'cause we got to live like animals.

GRANDMA. Here I come…into the kitchen…

HARRIET. Here she come into the kitchen…

GRANDMA. Hope I don't see nothin' an old woman ain't s'posed to see…

HARRIET. *(jumping off of* **TOM***'s lap)* What you not s'posed to see Grandma? Tell me, so I'll be sure not to be doin' it next time you go to the shed for four minutes.

GRANDMA. Tom hadn't you better be goin' now? Gettin' close to sundown.

TOM. Yes'm. Can I just have one kiss to hold me in the fields next week?

GRANDMA. 'Course you can.

> *(***TOM** *looks as though he's walking to* **HARRIET** *for a last embrace, steps past her and sweeps* **GRANDMA** *into a dip, kissing her loudly on the cheek.)*

TOM. Be seein' you ladies.

GRANDMA. You be careful de Paddy Rollers don't getchu.

> *(***TOM** *exits.)*

GRANDMA. *(to* **HARRIET***:)* He a mess.

HARRIET. 'Bout the prettiest, nicest, most hardworking mess this side the Mississippi, an he chose me.

GRANDMA. I'm glad to see you lettin' your heart go for a change.

HARRIET. I didn't let it go, he jes' grabt a hold of it faster'n I could keep it. You know the Master won't let us.

GRANDMA. Yes. But you got to let Tom be a man and try.

> *(***TOM** *pokes his head back in the door.)*

TOM. Almost forgot. Grandma, it alright wit' you if I ask Harriet for her hand?

GRANDMA. Wha' chu think Tom?

TOM. How 'bout Harriet, you give me your blessing to go to Master Norcom and ask for your hand?

> *(***HARRIET** *runs and hugs him.)*

HARRIET. You have my blessing! Always did…now go, fo' your overseer make it so you cain't come back.

> *(***TOM** *exits. Light rises on* **HAROLD SKINMORE** *[***ENSEMBLE***].)*

HAROLD. I's always big, like my daddy, and 'cause of it, d'overseer use me ta do his wuppin'. He say, "Harrolll commere," an han' me de whip and yell me to keep goin' 'til he say stop. Las' week I kilt Sam an' Nancy's girl, couldna been mo den twelve. Didn' mean to. He jes keep sayin, "Give her 'nether," an I has to do it. I don wan do it. I has to. Or it be me get beat. I cain't get a wife, cain't have no friends 'cause of it. Truly, I ain't a bad person. Truly I ain't.

Scene Three

(HARRIET and MARY scrub the floor and talk.)

HARRIET. And they was so pretty... I gone have a little girl some day. It jes...it made me sad Mary.

MARY. I don't see was so sad 'bout that.

HARRIET. It's the way little girls play together.

MARY. And...

HARRIET. And it broke my heart.

MARY. Hand me the rinse pail. Way I see it, your heart break too easy. You ain't gone live to see twenty-five.

HARRIET. Why I wanna live to be an old lady anyway?

(The very pregnant MISTRESS enters stage left and walks past. HARRIET and MARY scrub, never speaking, not taking their eyes off of her until she exits.)

MARY. I jes tellin' you. Your heart's too soff.

HARRIET. People always wanna confuse a soft heart for a soft soul. I'm jes fine thank you.

MARY. You welcome. You see Tom lately?

HARRIET. Why you ask?

MARY. You get tired of him, you let me know... I could make him very happy.

HARRIET. You a mess. See, this what I mean. These girls, what I seen in the field, was playin' like they do before they get like us, an' let a man make them jealous. They ain't thinkin' 'bout how pretty they look or tryin' to impress a boy. They jes lovin' each other and the day and the moment.

MARY. Whas this?

(MARY points to a spot on the floor. HARRIET leans over and scrapes the mark with her thumbnail.)

HARRIET. Thas from those new shoes Mistress got from Paris. They paint the soles black.

MARY. Well them fashionable shoes gonna get us a whippin' fa sho'.

> *(Both girls stop their talking and scrub furiously. It's a frantic, frightened scrubbing. Finally, the spot is removed. Both are relieved.)*

HARRIET. It was a little white girl and a little slave girl.

MARY. What?

HARRIET. What I was sayin…

MARY. Das right…

HARRIET. You know I don't put much stock into yellow hair and blue eyes, but this girl cute, all pink cheeks and dimples and curls. And the other's the kind of pretty I wouldn't wish on no slave girl. She be lucky she keep her virtue 'til she twelve bein' that pretty. Red brown, long curly braids and dimples too. Probly they sisters. But I know they only got 'bout two more years to love each other an' be friends, fo they know the truth.

MARY. It probly only be bad fo the niggra gal.

HARRIET. 'Course it worse for her, but the other one gone lose her best friend the day she know she own her best friend. And then, maybe five years later, they both look each other in the face real good and know the truth 'bout who they daddy is. An' it won't make no difference.

MARY. 'cept probbly the mistress sell her long 'fore that.

HARRIET. You ain't said a word. Don't wish pretty on no one.

MARY. You pretty, an' I ain't half bad myself.

HARRIET. That's why we in de big house, but you know there's some prettier an' smarter'n me. Heard 'bout that girl down on the Simms place? Took a flatiron to her own face ta keep de Massa an' his sons away from her.

MARY. I told you 'bout that.

HARRIET. I'll get the fresh water.

MARY. Thas all right. I finished here. I'll put back the furniture and do the entryway if you bleach and boil the diapers.

HARRIET. That lye bleach eat the skin off my fingers.

MARY. Poor Harriet. Maybe try fo'teen hours picken an' shuckin' come an' talk to me 'bout your hands.

HARRIET. I sorry Mary. I forget you got ta work outside too.

MARY. Don't pity me, jes don' be complainin' 'bout a little lye bleach.

(HARRIET finds a spot downstage right, as light fades on MARY furiously drying the floor.)

(HARRIET takes diapers off of a line and puts them in a large bucket, poking occasionally at them with a large stick. She sits on an upside down pail and pulls a small novel, from under her apron. The following is a round, each ENSEMBLE MEMBER repeating the passage HARRIET reads from the beginning.)

HARRIET. "Under the trees whose boughs made a friendly darkness, the amorous D'elmont throwing his eager arms round the virtuous Meloria's waist, placed burning kisses upon her neck,"

(MAN ENSEMBLE begins, whispering:)

MAN ENSEMBLE. "Under the trees whose..."

HARRIET. "creating in her, a kind of ecstasy,"

(FEMALE ENSEMBLE begins whispering the quote.)

HARRIET. "which might perhaps, had they been now alone, proved her desires were little different from his..."

(ENSEMBLE repeats, staggered, fading out as HARRIET continues to speak.)

HARRIET. Lost in the pages of a book I travel into exciting lands and become princesses and fair maidens. They always *fair*, but in my mind they look jes like me. In books I am beautiful and virtuous, well dressed, and always rescued by a handsome man who loves me for my beauty and my innate kindness. Innate kindness. I like the way that sounds. *(**HARRIET** closes the book.)* When I learned to read, it was my mistress before this one who taught me. The master's now dead sister. I do not think she taught me because she was particularly "virtuous" or *(beat)* "innately kind." I think she taught me because she was bored, as any sane woman resigned to a life of childbirth and frivolity would be. I also think she was not at all bright, and did not consider that once she taught me to read, I would then and forevermore, know how to read. It was as though my acquiring of each letter, each syllable, each phonetic advancement was an amusing miracle…but it had not occurred to her that those things might stay in my mind. Mistress Norcom would know better…

> *(**MISTRESS NORCOM** has approached **HARRIET** from behind.)*

You startled me Ma'am.

MISTRESS NORCOM. What are you doing?

HARRIET. *(still holding the book)* Bleaching the diapers.

MISTRESS NORCOM. Hand me that.

> *(**HARRIET** "innocently" offers the bucket of diapers.* ***MISTRESS NORCOM*** *slaps her and gestures to the book.)*

Not only does she read, an act punishable by death, but she reads garbage. What will the good doctor do when I tell him?

> *(**HARRIET** assumes an exaggerated "slave" dialect.)*

HARRIET. I's so sorry. Please may I goes back to my work?

MISTRESS NORCOM. Perhaps he'll finally give you the flogging you deserve and send you to the auction block.

HARRIET. It true, the Hacketts comin' by at noon? I really oughta make haste and lay out de table *(beat)* so's it bees ready for dem.

MISTRESS NORCOM. You seein' that black field nigga from the Stewart Plantation?

HARRIET. Don't know watchu mean ma'am?

MISTRESS NORCOM. Stop acting dumb and answer me plain. Have you been spending time with that black boy from the Stewarts' place?

HARRIET. Most de slaves on de Stewarts' plantation black.

MISTRESS NORCOM. Jes' know that the blackest one came shufflin' up to the back of the house this mornin' asking for an audience with the Master. The Doctor and I were just getting settled at the breakfast table. I answer the door and says, "And what is this regarding?"

(*A light rises on another area where we see "The Massa" and* **TOM.** *The scenes overlap.*)

MISTRESS NORCOM. And he says,

TOM & MISTRESS NORCOM. If it please you jes as much,

TOM. I'd like to make my business wit de Massa hisself.

MISTRESS NORCOM. Says it just like that,

TOM. (*groveling*) Wit de Massa hisself.

MISTRESS NORCOM. Don't seem like the way a boy spend time with our Harriet would say it, but he takes off his hat, and lowers his head and says those insulting words to me just like that. "Wit de Massa hisself."

TOM. If it please the Mistress, I would be most grateful if I may speak with the Master alone.

MISTRESS NORCOM. Just like I am too stupid to smell the insult. As though he might as well say…

TOM. Cain't do my business with you, you ain't nothing but a foolish gal. You ain't no good for nothin' but warmin' the bed and havin' babies.

MISTRESS NORCOM. So I say, you wait just right here.

(**MISTRESS NORCOM** *steps into the scene.*)

MISTRESS NORCOM. *And* I get the good Doctor, and I stand behind his left shoulder, because of course, now I want to know, what business does this dirty nigra have that's too important for my female ears. And he pulls out a filthy envelope with at least seven hundred greasy dollar bills in it and says,

TOM & MISTRESS NORCOM. If it please de Massa

MISTRESS NORCOM. He in love wit a servant girl…

TOM. …and I know the askin' price be somewhere in de fambly of five hunded. But I know de servant been in dis here family a long time, so I sweetened the deal wit two mo' hunded,

MISTRESS NORCOM & TOM. and would de kind Massa…

TOM. …see in his heart fo to let me buy her into freedom wit' de money I earned for my own freedom, so's I might marry her, and live outside of sin 'til such a time as my own good Massa see his way to let me buy my freedom.

(Light fades on TOM and Massa.)

MISTRESS NORCOM. First I think, how a field nigga get that kind of money…

HARRIET. He a carpenter. Hire himself out on his off time…

MISTRESS NORCOM. Shut up that mouth. And then I think, this is a good day. Truly a glorious day. I will have extra pocket change, and be rid of lazy Harriet, all at once. And may I share what the Good Doctor does then?

(Light rises again.)

He counts each and every one of those dirty bills, twice. And he says,

MASTER NORCOM. Which property is it you're so in love with as to give up your own freedom?

TOM. Harriet sir.

MISTRESS NORCOM. And my husband walks into the kitchen, throws the money in the fire, and says,

MASTER NORCOM. I'll sell her to you for eight hundred and fifty and not a penny less

MASTER & MISTRESS NORCOM. on the day hell freezes over.

(Light out on **DOCTOR** *and* **TOM**.*)*

MISTRESS NORCOM. I only tell you this because you are like family to me. And so, if we are to put up with one another for the rest of eternity, let it be understood. I will tolerate no more insolence. I will not be reminded of the skills my dear stupid sister-in-law imparted to you before her unfortunate demise. And I will not have you skulking about with my husband. *(pause)* Understood.

HARRIET. Yes.

MISTRESS NORCOM. I did not hear you clearly. You said?

HARRIET. Yes ma'am.

MISTRESS NORCOM. Now please get the table laid and make sure the cook has prepared a lunch for eight. We musn't appear unready for the Hacketts. Are you crying?

HARRIET. No ma'am.

MISTRESS NORCOM. I didn't think so.

(Lights out. Up immediately on:)

Scene Four

(A WORKER *steps forward.* HARRIET *hears his story as she crosses into* GRANDMA*'s kitchen.)*

JOSHUA (ENSEMBLE). Name's Joshua. I don' git beat. Firs time Massah tried ta lay hand on me, I grabbed his whip, looked him in de eyes an' say, "I's a crazy niggah. I'll work hard fo you, pick twice much as any demo work wit out complainin'. Mate wit anyone you wan' match me wit. But chu hit me, I'll kill you an' anyone I can take to hell wit me fo dey kill me firs. Been here fifteen yeahs, sired gone on eighteen youngins, most sold time dey was three, pick three times mo den de res, an ain' never been lashed by none 'em. Don' s'pose I evah will.

(Lights fade on JOSHUA, *rise as* HARRIET *enters* GRANDMA*'s kitchen.)*

HARRIET. It's been three weeks. He ain't comin' back is he?

GRANDMA. Is that my good morning?

HARRIET. Sorry. He ain't comin' back?

GRANDMA. How many times you gone ask?

HARRIET. Why I try make him marry me? We coulda gone on like we was…maybe do like others an' even make babies.

GRANDMA. You know I love Tom. But you still jes a girl. An if he cain't find the man in him to show his face, you the better for it. There's other men.

HARRIET. Maybe it is time for me to run…

GRANDMA. Hush. You run, get yourself killed or worse, *(beat)* I'll kill you myself. I got a hen lays when she feels like it… I think she'll fry up nice.

HARRIET. What I'm s'posed to do?

GRANDMA. Girl, you need to cry for five minutes and be about your business. Mind the shop for me for jes a minute, got a hen to strangle.

*(*GRANDMA *exits, re-enters)*

And your five minutes was up 'bout ten days ago.

(GRANDMA exits. HARRIET removes her work apron and wipes a counter top. SAMUEL TREADWELL SAWYER, a "white" gentleman enters.)

SAWYER. Good evening.

HARRIET. Yes sir.

SAWYER. Afternoon really.

HARRIET. Yes sir. *(long pause)* Is there something I may help you with?

SAWYER. That depends.

(long pause)

HARRIET. Yes sir?

SAWYER. Only if you will do me the honor of looking at me.

HARRIET. I don't understand.

SAWYER. I feel I am competing with your shoes. Are they very special?

HARRIET. My shoes?

SAWYER. Do you find your shoes more interesting than I?

HARRIET. I don't know. How interesting do you find my shoes?

SAWYER. *(laughing)* Do you find your shoes more interesting than I am?

HARRIET. I don't know you. My shoes are safe. And predictable. And will not accuse me of impudence if I look at them.

SAWYER. I should like a half-dozen sourdough rolls, please.

HARRIET. *(still not looking up)* Yes sir.

SAWYER. What is your favorite?

HARRIET. It depends on the day.

SAWYER. The quality of the baked goods changes daily?

HARRIET. No sir. My preferences change daily.

SAWYER. My name is Samuel Treadwell Sawyer.

HARRIET. Yes sir.

SAWYER. Have you a name?

HARRIET. Yes sir. *(beat)* Just the rolls then?

SAWYER. Something sweet.

HARRIET. Grandmother makes a nice shortbread with just a touch of jam in the middle.

SAWYER. Then a dozen please.

> (**HARRIET** *busies herself putting the baked goods in a basket. The gentleman is more and more intrigued.* **HARRIET** *has still not made eye contact.*)

SAWYER. Do you live here?

HARRIET. You must be new in town then?

SAWYER. Yes and no. My family has been here for some time, the Sawyer Estate. I've recently returned from the north, where I practiced law. *(beat)* So, I ask again. Do you live here?

HARRIET. No sir. My grandmother is free and owns this house and business. I belong on the Norcom plantation, down the road.

SAWYER. Your Grandmother is not here?

HARRIET. My Grandmother will be here shortly.

SAWYER. You speak very well.

HARRIET. Thank you, so do you.

SAWYER. You seem sad…

> (**HARRIET** *meets his gaze for the first time.*)

HARRIET. It shows?

SAWYER. Well then how much do I owe you?

> (**GRANDMOTHER** *enters, hand around the neck of the dead hen. She crosses quickly to examine the contents in the basket.*)

GRANDMA. Five cents for the rolls, ten for the shortbread. Five for the basket if you ain't bringin' it back.

HARRIET. And one for the lemon snickerdoodle.

SAWYER. *(amused)* Snickerdoodle…?

GRANDMA. She is fifteen.

SAWYER. I am only asking for furture...

HARRIET. My preference *(beat)* today.

SAWYER. Well thank you. And thank your grandmother for me.

GRANDMA. You may thank me yourself.

SAWYER. What is your granddaughter's name?

GRANDMA. She belongs to the Norcom plantation... *(beat)* Would there be anything else for you then?

SAWYER. No, thank you ma'am. I will bring back the basket. Pleasant day then.

> (**SAWYER** *hands* **HARRIET** *the money,* **GRANDMOTHER** *intercepts and pockets it. He exits.*)

HARRIET. He seems nice enough.

GRANDMA. A "nice" white man's more dangerous than a mean one.

HARRIET. Why?

GRANDMA. This is my experience. *(pause)* There are things I should have told you, about men and women...

HARRIET. I know about relations.

GRANDMA. You know?

HARRIET. I've heard.

GRANDMA. You must not leave yourself open to men who will degrade you. *(pause)* Has the Master ever laid a hand on you?

HARRIET. No ma'am.

GRANDMA. Has he ever asked you for extra favors?

HARRIET. Grandma surely you know the Master is bigger and stronger and if he wants...

GRANDMA. I'm talking about the stupid girl who thinks her body a bargaining chip for an easier life. It's never the case. Because your body and soul are not valued by the men who ask for it.

HARRIET. You heard about Rose Cabarrison? Her young master fell in love with her and freed her and her children and her mammy too.

GRANDMA. And you think that's freedom?

HARRIET. A little house on the edge of town look like freedom to me.

GRANDMA. That little house ain't on the edge of town, that house on the edge of the Cabarisson Plantation. 'Sides, it look like a slave cabin wit' a coat of white paint and flowers in the yard to me. You look inside that house, you'd see they not free.

HARRIET. I don't understand...

GRANDMA. I made myself a trade of baking, 'stead of making myself the trade. I can bake even now that I ain't so much to look at. I can bake and earn my own keep never mind the whims of some man with a family to support and no legal reason to stay true.

HARRIET. I promise, I would never compromise myself.

GRANDMA. Thas all I ask. You stay ignorant to his advances, stay near the mistress and the kids. You be the good girl I have raised you to be.

HARRIET. Yes ma'am.

GRANDMA. 'Cept on your wedding night...

HARRIET. Grandma...

GRANDMA. Don't be a good girl on your wedding night. Wedding beds are made for fun. I bore your grandfather three healthy babies from a loving bed...

HARRIET. You had six children...

GRANDMA. I bore your grandfather three. *(sobering beat)* You understand?

HARRIET. Yes Ma'am.

GRANDMA. Good.

HARRIET. You really think I'll marry one day?

GRANDMA. Don't see why not. You young, you pretty, you can almost cook *(beat)* and *(she thinks...)* well, that's enough. You just need a good boy from this plantation, so's it don't require nothin' but a nod from the Master. Put on a pot of grease so we can send some of this bird home with you 'fore dark.

(Lights fade.)

Scene Five

(Light rises on MARY.)

MARY. Is jest the usual I guess. I work in de big house in de first of summer an' thru de winter. Other times I harvest de hay and de corn. Don' have ta pick cotton. Massa's brother came up to visit wit' his nephew. His nephew jes turn thirteen. I fifteen. Massa an' his brother decide I what dey gone give de nephew fo his birfday. Not to have, jes to use. I gone spare you de ress.

(Light fades on MARY, rises on HARRIET. HARRIET to audience...)

HARRIET. Sometimes I wish he'd just force me like he do the others. But I'm special.

(Light rises on MASTER, then MARY. The following are three separate scenes that overlap in time and space.)

MISTRESS NORCOM. You act like she's special James. She's just a slave girl.

MASTER NORCOM. You're special, Harriet.

MARY. Ack like you think you so special.

HARRIET. I ain't listenin' to that Mary. *(to MASTER)* You be needin' anything else this evening sir?

MASTER NORCOM. You know what I need.

HARRIET. Then, I jes be getting back to Miss Lizzie Mae and Junior then.

MASTER NORCOM. Why don' you come over here for a minute, Harriet.

(Light rises on MISTRESS NORCOM.)

MISTRESS. Harriet, I know the Master put you in a new room at the end of the hall, but I want you to fix yourself up a pallet and sleep in the nursery with Lizzie Mae and Junior, cross the hall from me.

HARRIET. Massa, Lizzie Mae been having bad dreams lately, maybe you wan' me to go back to her, 'case she wake up distressed.

MASTER NORCOM. I want you to consider how sweet I could make your life.

HARRIET. My life alright now. *(beat)* Thank you.

MASTER NORCOM. Your hands are rough, dark circles under your eyes, your clothes always stained and dirty. Think how nice your life could be if you lived in your own place, and wore a pretty dress and had only yourself and your children to care for.

HARRIET. I don't have children.

MASTER. But you could. Pretty ones too.

HARRIET. Tom and I…

MASTER. Shut your mouth about that boy nigger! He ain't havin' nothin' more to do with you. Now come over here. Now!

    (HARRIET steps back.)

MASTER. Why do you always cower in my presence. I am a kind man. Am I not? *(raises his hand as if to slap her)* Answer me?

HARRIET, MISTRESS, MARY. Yes.

HARRIET. Yes sir, you are.

MASTER. I have never forced myself upon you, and I never will.

HARRIET. Thank you sir.

MASTER. But, you are foolish to ignore my… *(beat)* attention. Do you think you're better than the rest of them?

MARY. Sometime you act like you think you better'n the rest of us.

HARRIET. No.

MARY. You do.

HARRIET. I don't mean to.

MARY. How long you think it is 'fo he have his way by force and be through wit you. He'd sell you down the river fo you could even get your drawers up.

HARRIET. That's ugly.

MARY. Life's ugly. Some of us don't get to say no.

HARRIET. Oh, Mary… I didn't know…

MARY. Jes sayin'…

MASTER. Where do you go when I'm talking to you Harriet?

HARRIET. I'm right here.

MISTRESS. I see you there. Surely you have somethin' to attend to.

HARRIET. Yes. *(to* **MASTER***)* I should get back to the…

MASTER. I could have anyone these slave girls I want and I've chosen you. But you haven't even the sense to be grateful.

MARY. Maybe you should shut up, cooperate and be grateful.

HARRIET. Were you?

MISTRESS. James, we lost another field slave in birth today. Overseer says she had a white baby.

MASTER. That's not possible. Black can't have white.

MISTRESS. But it seems white can have blacks all over this plantation.

HARRIET. I don't think I'm better.

MASTER. Watch your mouth…

(Again the **MASTER** *raises his hand as if to strike.)*

(All three **WOMEN** *flinch instinctively.)*

MISTRESS. That dirty little wench, act like she thinks she's better than I.

HARRIET. Mary, I don't, I don't think I'm better. It's just my body won't let me do it. He hate us, I don't understand why he even want that. Really, I think I would be sick. He older than Grandma, and smell like death.

MISTRESS. Always lookin' like she smell somethin' bad. Tell me, how can a slave look like that.

MASTER. Who?

MISTRESS. Harriet.

HARRIET. I think I hear Mistress callin' .

MASTER. *(to* **HARRIET***)* She's nothing for you to worry about. *(to* **MISTRESS NORCOM***)* Surely you have distractions, something to keep your mind off of vulgar things.

HARRIET & MISTRESS. I think I hear the children,

HARRIET. I should…

MASTER. I've ordered a house to be built down in the bottoms, behind the corn crops. You will live there, by yourself, no more visits to your Grandma. I will tell the Mistress and the townspeople you are there to tend to the vegetable garden and teach the slave children scripture. You will live there and I will visit when I please. *(beat)* What do you have to say?

HARRIET. Only that I should die first…

MASTER. "Only that I should die first" what? …

HARRIET. Only that I should die first, sir.

MASTER. And when I visit, I shall be received with open arms.

(Lights fade on **MISTRESS***,* **MASTER***, and* **MARY***.)*

HARRIET. *(to audience)* If I could make it all stop, but it won't. If it was just voices in my head, but it's real, and I can't make it stop. It won't stop. It never stops.

(Light fades on **HARRIET***, rises on* **GRANDMA***, kneading bread.)*

GRANDMA. Cookin' for de big house was a blessing an a curse. A blessing 'cause you can feed your kids wit de scraps an you always know everthin' 'bout wass happenin'. But dat's de curse too. See de Massah an' Missus take deir breakfas in de kitchen, 'way from de kids, an dat's where dey talk business an such. An' you jess a piece a furniture what makes de food. Dey be sayin' things like "Gotta cow on de Avery plantation I had ta order put down, she too ole, and speakin' a old, Jessie gettin' up there an ain't been pickin' his quota, you know Jessie?" An' de Missus say, "You know I cain't hardly tell any de niggahs apart, specially not them blue black field hands," an' de Massah say, "Well, don't know if its bettah to have Jim Perkins ride him harder, if I make more to sell him at a loss, or maybe best we put him out all our misery. An I gatta say, you wan' more gravey fa yo biscuits ma'am? Sir?"

Scene Six

>(**HARRIET**, **MARY** and **GRANDMOTHER** in **GRANDMOTHER**'s kitchen. It has been ransacked. They stand in the middle looking at the damage...)

HARRIET. We'll clean it up Grandma...you see...we'll make it all right.

GRANDMA. Ain't no "all right." I know it ain't Nat's fault... but Lawd...

MARY. Who you talkin' bout?

GRANDMA. Nat Turner...

HARRIET. He a slave what started a revolt, got all the white folks scared...

MARY. Oh...

>(**MARY** starts to laugh)

That's why Mistress been so jumpy. I jes looked at her an' she liked to jump outta her skin, thought she'd drop that baby right there on the floor.

HARRIET. They didn't hurt you did they?

GRANDMA. No sweetie. They jes take what they want, say they searchin' fo evidence of insurrection.

MARY. Insurrection?

HARRIET. Like Grandma got guns and gone go outta her head and start killin' white folks.

MARY. You think that'd be a bad idea?

>(The **WOMEN** begin putting the room in order.)

GRANDMA. You shouldn't say that out loud. *(to **MARY**)* It's just these poor whites what cain't afford slaves workin' out they anger. But it's funny, 'cause wouldn't chu think I could jes put glass in these crackers and kill the whole damn town in one fell swoop. Come in here, eat my food while they tear up my house lookin' for somethin' I might use to hurt them.

MARY. That's crazy.

GRANDMA. That's worse than crazy, that's stupid. Mary, get me a mop... Harriet, you see cain't you get these things back on the shelf... I gotta...

(*Door opens,* **SAMUEL TREADWELL SAWYER** *enters.*)

SAWYER. Good afternoon ladies.

GRANDMA. Afternoon. Can I help you?

SAWYER. (*to* **HARRIET**) How are you this fine day Miss Harriet?

GRANDMA. I said, can I help you?

SAWYER. Came to bring back the basket like I promised. (*beat – noticing the state of the place*) Perhaps I've come at an inconvenient time?

HARRIET. (*taking basket*) Thank you Massa Sawyer.

SAWYER. Please, call me Massa Samuel. Or just Samuel. (*to* **GRANDMOTHER**) Came to talk to Harriet for a moment ma'am. Jes a minute of her time outside, I promise no harm. Maybe while we talk, you'll fill that basket up. See it comes to three dollars.

MARY. Three?!

(**GRANDMOTHER** *drags* **HARRIET** *to the side.*)

GRANDMA. You remember what I told you.

HARRIET. Yes ma'am.

MARY. (*to* **GENTLEMAN**) *Maybe* I can, help you Massa Samuel?

SAWYER. Thank you, I'll wait for Harriet.

HARRIET. (*to audience*) Some choices not choices.

SAWYER. You like horses Harriet?

(*beat*)

MARY. They alright when you need to get to someplace quick and...

HARRIET. Least they don't seem like choices when you're in the middle of it all. (*to* **SAWYER**) Yes. I do. Like horses. They're pretty and gentle and have noses like velvet. (*to* *audience)* Noses like velvet? *(to* **SAWYER***)* Soft noses, that feel like...

SAWYER. Velvet. I agree. Got a new filly, a little chocolate and blonde palamino. Maybe I can show you sometime. *(pause)* She's real gentle.

HARRIET. *(to audience)* How do I help you understand?

SAWYER. You'll come? I can drop you off at the Norcoms' after.

HARRIET. *(to audience)* Please do not think less of me.

SAWYER. Shouldn't take us a more than a few minutes out the way.

> *(***HARRIET** *lets* **SAWYER** *guide her out of the store, he exits as she speaks to audience.)*

HARRIET. If I may explain. *(beat)* Living the life of chattel. Truly it is, indescribable. But not describing it would make our time together futile, so still I try.

> *(***ENSEMBLE** *members step forward one at a time to "help.")*

TOM. Maybe we should tell you 'bout the plantation where they hang a slave from the ceiling.

HAROLD. They build a fire on a screen over him, and put a ham on the fire.

TOM. The hot drippings fall and burn the skin of the poor victim, until he is killed or scarred forever.

HARRIET. But you see, this is not what I want tell you. None of this is new to your sensitive ears. It is how you must put your feet in the shoes of the person who has to cut the burnt man down, or in the shoes of the wife who must tend to his burns or bury him, or the children who bring him water and smell the burning flesh, so he stay alive through his torture.

ENSEMBLE (FEMALE). Maybe we should tell you 'bout how if you get caught stealin' once they whip you good, twice they put you in the shed and no food or water for a week, three times and they might cut off one or two fingers.

ENSEMBLE (FEMALE). They usually leave the hand 'cause you got to have it to hold a shovel or a hoe.

HARRIET. But you've heard about that. Or at least something like it.

ENSEMBLE (MALE). Maybe we should tell you 'bout how they tie a third time runner to four horses. One arm for one horse, one leg for another… Den they set those horses running all in different directions.

HARRIET. But again, this is not what I wish to tell you. I do not mean to upset you…only to help you understand. It's the nigra groomsmen who have to round' up the horses and untie the victim's severed limbs. It is the wives of the groomsmen who have to hold their husbands while they tell the story at night.

GRANDMA. It's the countless women and children who must walk over the blood stained earth to get to the fields the next day.

HARRIET. It's even the children of the Master and Misses who must hear the screams and witness such atrocities.

GRANDMA. What you must understand is that it is in the air.

ENSEMBLE (FEMALE). You can smell it.

HARRIET. You taste it.

ENSEMBLE (MALE). Cain't wash it off your skin. Cain't get it out your hair. It stays under your nails with the earth.

ENSEMBLE (MALE). It is in your body and mind.

GRANDMA. It is in the soil.

MARY. In the water. In the rags we call clothes.

HARRIET. When there is no law that protects you. When your momma and daddy cannot protect you. When your own wits will never be a match for a life that puts you always at the mercy of others.

ENSEMBLE (FEMALE). It is the way it is,

ENSEMBLE (MALE). The way it feel from here…
 the way it will always be,

ENSEMBLE (FEMALE). and we see it

ENSEMBLE (MALE). and we feel it and

ALL. we live it.

> *(One by one, members of the* **ENSEMBLE** *step forward, eventually obscuring her. They are singing a heartbreaking, quiet, soulful hymn.)*
>
> *(***HARRIET,*** now behind the crowd, steps forward. She is pregnant and holds a baby.)*

HARRIET. And this is why you must forgive me my choice.

> *(Their singing is devoid of emotion and obvious sadness, for the words are sad enough.)*
>
> *(Lights fade.)*

End of ACT I

ACT II

Scene One

*(Light rises on **MARY**, and a very pregnant **HARRIET** scrubbing the floor. They take a moment to admire the baby in the Moses basket between them.)*

MARY. *(talking to baby)* Him de hansmest thing…aren'chu… Aren'chu.

HARRIET. It's hard Mary…don' know sleep at all no more. Mistress all time given me the back hand if he be cryin'…when the milk come in, they got hard an' it hurt, an' hurt eben more when he first start to suckling.

MARY. Granny didn' help you?

HARRIET. I ain't ask.

MARY. It all bad?

HARRIET. No. Look at him.

(They gaze at the baby.)

Didn't know I could feel this way for anything. He have a holt of my heart more even then Tom did. I jes didn't know it'd be like this.

MARY. *(to **HARRIET**)* Cain't b'lieve de Mistress eben let chu stay here…dis baby prettier den anything she ever had.

HARRIET. I'm sure it's not the Mistress let me stay, I think the Massa do, but I don' know why.

MARY. Why you don' leave de baby which yo granny?

HARRIET. Cain't.

MARY. Ya'll still ain't speakin'?

HARRIET. She think these the Massa's babies.

MARY. Das what everybody think…

HARRIET. Not everybody. Massa knows better. Still, better Grandma think the massa forced me. I cain't have her know I laid down with Massa Samuel of my own free will…

MARY. Ain' nothin' bout you free.

HARRIET. So I cain't go near her, she look in my eyes and she know.

MARY. Why she cain't know?

HARRIET. I made her a promise an' I broke it. Sides, Massa won't let me go there no more. *(beat)* He do treat me nice enuf though.

MARY. Who?

HARRIET. Baby's father.

MARY. Massa Samuel Sawyer?

HARRIET. Yes.

MARY. He treat you so good, why you still here?

*(Offended, **HARRIET** turns her back to **MARY** and works on the floor.)*

MARY. I didn't mean no harm. Jes seem like he white, an rich, an powerful, so must be he can do whatever he want, why he not jes come up and ride away wit' you on a horse.

HARRIET. That'd be stealin, and he cain't jes come out an ask Massa to sell me. You know Massa never do that. I figure now Massa see I have two, with the same father, he be so mad he'll put me on the block fo sho, den dey Daddy can come buy me.

*(**MASTER NORCOM** enters.)*

MASTER NORCOM. Sell you fo sho, why?

*(**HARRIET** and **MARY** put their heads down and scrub.)*

MASTER NORCOM. Mary, you excuse us for minute?

MARY. Missus be on me with a switch she sees me gone.

MASTER NORCOM. Then she'll have to be on you. GO!

> *(MARY runs out. HARRIET keeps scrubbing. Instinctively protecting her pregnant belly.)*

MASTER NORCOM. You're still not talking to me? After I caught your little white baby? You still have nothing to say to me after I gave you a bed to rest up in for a day after the birth?

> *(HARRIET stops scrubbing. She sits quietly for a long moment, finely meeting the MASTER'S gaze.)*

HARRIET. Thank you Massa. Thank you for everything.

MASTER NORCOM. I have given you four years to come round. You think I'm gone just walk around sniffin' after you the rest of my life. You think I'm gone build you that house so some other man's baby can live off of my money while you act like a white lady. You forget who you are. You forget who I am. I have no intentions of putting you on the block. I think instead I'll wait 'til you have this next an' sell my new properties, together. May I?

> *(The MASTER picks up the baby in the basket. Holds it carelessly.)*

Mulatto slave babies bring a good price. Some little girl somewhere will be happy for a live babe to play with. Or maybe I should wait until they are eight or nine and sell them into hard labor. I just have to think about it. Perhaps it depends entirely upon how you choose to behave.

HARRIET. Please.

MASTER NORCOM. Please what Harriet?

HARRIET. Please sir. My baby.

> *(The MASTER drops the baby, HARRIET catches it. Lights fade as ENSEMBLE sings a lullaby.)*

Scene Two

MALE ENSEMBLE. I wan' show you sumpin I carry wif me. Is what dey call a bill o' sale fo my Daddy. Dat's de papers go wit you when you get put on de block. Fount it in a box under my mama's bed when she past. Cain't read, but I knowd some o' what it say, my mama knowed it, tolt it to me. Say some'n 'bout dis here nigra, Moses, solt to so's and so, on such n' such a date fo de 'mount of sebbenty-fibe dollars, an dis here de part I like: It say – Moses, a strong buck wif a good manner, dark black skin, an good teef. Put it in dis pouch wear roun' my neck, make me feel close to him.

> (**HARRIET** *enters...no longer pregnant, she carries a toddler strapped to her back and now an infant strapped to her front. A bag of provisions, a canteen, and a hat hang from her shoulders and around her neck. She's dressed to run. She addresses audience.*)

HARRIET. I would not wish to presume that my enslaved comrades visited thoughts of running as often as I... though it is hard to imagine one wouldn't. Every bush, every rock, gully, or tree seems to offer shelter for an unplanned escape. But they are hollow offerings, as nature has provided little protection from the noses of the hounds and the ruthless desperation of hungry slave catchers. The night I birthed my girl, the Master made clear his intentions to no longer torment me with threats. That he should not only make good on his promises, but sell my children as far away as possible. Friends and allies harbored me in attics and basements, the Master and his bloodhounds always at our heels. Almost as much as I feared my own capture, I feared for the safety of my brave and loyal friends who would most certainly be put to death for harboring me. This drove me finally into the woods.

(A haunting lullaby is sung by a far away **FEMALE** *cast member it becomes a rhythmic chorus, as, in silhouette we see a depiction of* **HARRIET***'s escape, helped by the* **ENSEMBLE***.)*

(As the song drifts back into a melodic strain, a light rises on **HARRIET** *standing in* **GRANDMA***'s doorway, severely disheveled and feverish.)*

*(***GRANDMA** *goes to her, pulls her in. They hug,* **GRANDMA** *rocks* **HARRIET** *as she clings to her and sobs. Lights fade.)*

Scene Three

*(Light rises on **HARRIET** holding a baby, another in a basket at her feet. **GRANDMOTHER** tends to **HARRIET**'s many bites and abrasions. She places a damp cloth over a snake bite on her leg.)*

GRANDMA. You lucky it wasn't a cotton-mouth…

HARRIET. Ow…

GRANDMA. You still feverish… I think it's infection, not venom. This should draw it out.

HARRIET. I shouldn't have put the babies through it, Grandma, the mosquitoes were worse than the snakes…

GRANDMA. …and the babies didn't cry?

HARRIET. Not once.

GRANDMA. Thas' a miracle.

HARRIET. Well, I give each a finger dipped in honey an moonshine, hid in the marshes, but my milk was dryin' up fast. I even thought 'bout runnin' to Tom, but I was scared of the Paddy Rollers and the overseers…

GRANDMA. Ya shoulda been more scared of Tom's wife then the overseers…

HARRIET. *(chuckling)* I thought of that too.

*(They sit in silence for a moment. **HARRIET** puts the baby to her breast.)*

GRANDMA. Harriet. You would run and not come say bye to your old granny?

HARRIET. I thought better that than you know the truth.

GRANDMA. Girl, I saw the truth coming minute that Massa Samuel walk in here talkin' 'bout, was your name…

HARRIET. I promised.

GRANDMA. I was wrong to ask you to. Grandma know how it be, an I sorry. I so sorry I ask more of you than the world let you be. You a good girl 'cause you got a good heart, an a good mind, an what between those strong legs of yours, an who go there don' make you less.

HARRIET. What I gone do?

> *(The men in the* **ENSEMBLE** *sing a work song as they set up the shed we saw at the top of the play.)*

GRANDMA. You cain't stay here, this the first place they come lookin'. I been thinkin' on this. I know how you don't much like tight places. But there a little space, right under the rafters, behind the chimney, up in the shed. You hide up there. Jes' for a spell. Jes 'til he get tired of lookin' for you an' we figure out how we get you north.

HARRIET. Me and the babies?

GRANDMA. You know you cain't run with two babies.

HARRIET. You right, but I cain't run without them, they a piece of me.

GRANDMA. Then seems you have a choice to make. But you best be thinkin' 'bout that where you safe from harm. Now that you decided to start runnin' you cain't go back…

HARRIET. An' I wouldn't, not for nothin'.

> *(Lights fade. The house servants work rhythms from earlier blends with the rhythms of the workers in the cotton field as they build* **HARRIET**'s *hiding place.)*

> *(We see* **HARRIET** *hand* **GRANDMA** *her babies.* **GRANDMA** *exits with them.* **HARRIET** *is alone. She climbs into her hiding space.)*

> *(blackout)*

Scene Four

(Light rises on **ISAAC**.*)*

ISAAC. Hadn't nebber seen dis kind a place for I come here. Worked for the Simms two counties over. They like most white folks, a small house, a shed, an two or three of us in a back room offa de kitchen. We's all hungry all de time, not jes us what work there, but the white folks what owns us too. Three years past, a draught kills off the Simms' wheat crop. First they sell my four-year-ole' girl, then three o' the five chickens, then my woman, then the mule what pulled de plow. I can pull good as the mule, *an'* use my hands. I don' get solt here 'til affer de Simms baby dies when de Missus milk dry up. It better here…don't know hunger no more, an always hab shoes on my feet.

(Light fades on **ISAAC**, *rises on* **HARRIET** *from her hiding space.)*

HARRIET. There is a blinding darkness. Darker than the brightest, whitest light. A deafening silence, that can hurt your ears with its complete absence of sound. And this is how it was. It is small, but even on the worse days, it is bigger than my world outside. This space bigger even then my world ever was or could be. An' maybe there room to breathe in the north, but maybe I cain't breathe without my children. Maybe this air will taint them more if I ain't here to protect them… This is how it was. And this is how it felt. And this not something easy to tell you.

(Light changes, it is as thought **HARRIET**'s *hiding space is illuminated from within.)*

*(***GRANDMA** *pokes her head in…)*

GRANDMA. You awake?

HARRIET. Always.

GRANDMA. You keep stretchin' those legs?

HARRIET. Best I can Grandma. How are the children?

GRANDMA. They sleep. Send me down your waste.

> (**HARRIET** *lowers a bucket on a rope. Through the following* **GRANDMA** *exchanges it for a basket of provisions and a fresh bucket.*)

HARRIET. Benny minding you? Ellen, she eating? You know how she get funny 'bout eating, it worry me she won't have enough fat on her bones to keep her warm through winter...

GRANDMA. They fine sweetie. How you feel?

HARRIET. Back hurt... But good Grandma. Truly. Maybe I stay here forever... I like Master think I ran north an I right here under his nose.

GRANDMA. I don' like this playin' with fire. You gone get found out an it be the end of our family.

HARRIET. No. NO ...I will not be found out. But I need your help...

GRANDMA. What I been doin' all these months?

HARRIET. Please... I been thinkin' on it an' I know what to do... I need several sheets of parchment paper, envelopes and sealing wax... *(beat)* an, this the part you not gone like... I need you get Massa Samuel to come by...

GRANDMA. Here?

HARRIET. I know...but I must speak with him. Please, just get him to agree to come by after sundown, don' tell him I here, jes' bring him an I will explain everything...

> (**GRANDMA** *does not respond.*)

You say you trust I have a good head, then trust me this. I will not be found out, I will not bring harm to you or the children. But I cannot leave them.

GRANDMA. You readin' that Bible I brung you?

HARRIET. I usin' it.

> (**GRANDMA***'s sent up the new provisions and begins to exit...*)

GRANDMA. I see you maybe day after tomorrow. Try please to move them bowels.

*(***GRANDMA** *exits.)*

HARRIET. I learned to read on the Bible. Not so exciting as my love and adventure stories, but it's a nice book to have read. I pray God understand how I use it now. The pages where I write, to keep my head out places where it ought not to be, and still my mind make the voices come…

MASTER NORCOM. I can smell you up there Harriet…

HARRIET. So I write…

MASTER NORCOM. Used to smell good, now I wouldn't want to touch you for the stench of that smell…

HARRIET. And I write…

MASTER NORCOM. The missus say she miss you. Say she ain't got no one to fill her mind with murderous thoughts. That keep her under my feet an' so, I miss you too.

HARRIET. Shut it!

*(***MASTER NORCOM** *disappears.)*

I tried writing stories for the children…but since Granny cain't read to 'em, that seem a waste of time and a little sad. So I write 'bout what I know. What I remember, way I want it to be, way I hope it be someday.

*(***HARRIET** *writes.)*

Scene Five

>(**HARRIET**'s writing. **TOM** appears out of nowhere.)

TOM. Watchu doin?

HARRIET. Tom...you scared me. *(beat)* Writing.

TOM. May I?

>(**HARRIET** hands **TOM** the book. **MASTER** reappears.)

MASTER NORCOM. I can smell you Harriet.

TOM. You want I kill him for you Harriet?

HARRIET. Thank you Tom, that'd be very thoughtful.

>(**MASTER NORCOM**'s light goes out...)

TOM. Says here you loved me more than you knew to tell me.

HARRIET. Yes.

TOM. Says, if you could, you would tell me now jes how much.

HARRIET. Yes Tom. I sorry I didn' know how to say it plain before.

TOM. Why you love me? Jes' 'cause I can read your words?

HARRIET. No Tom. I love you understand my words. I love you listen and so you hear my words and so you hear my heart. I love your brown hard arms, I love the hair on your chest, an the way your neck smell. I love the way I have to stand on my toes to smell that neck.

TOM. Thas real nice Harriet. You got anyone else you need kilt today?

HARRIET. No. Not today. Thank you.

>(**TOM**'s light fades.)

(to **TOM***)* Wait Tom...wait...

>(**TOM**'s light fades back up...)

TOM. Uhhuh...

HARRIET. Why you love me?

TOM. For your beauty an' your innate kindness.

HARRIET. *(to audience)* Afraid as I was of being discovered… my greatest fear was that I should come out of hiding without my mind.

(**GRANDMA** *enters.*)

GRANDMA. Harriet,

HARRIET. Tom?

GRANDMA. It's Grandma…been a week, come down for a moment and stretch those legs… Got the chillun playin on the front porch with Mary, lef the door open an' tells 'em I be right back, jes' gain to put on the potatoes fa' dinner.

(**HARRIET** *climbs down.*)

GRANDMA. I worry 'bout you up there all the time mumblin'. You really thought I might be Tom? …

HARRIET. 'Course not, I was mostly half asleep.

GRANDMA. Massa Sawyer 'roun back, …you want I bring him in?

(**SAMUEL** *emerges from shadows…*)

SAMUEL. Harriet?

HARRIET . Massa Samuel.

SAMUEL. You don't look well…

HARRIET. *(to* **GRANDMA***)* We'll be alright Grandma…

(**GRANDMA** *exits.*)

Forgive me please…lately I not so sure wha's really happenin', an' what's happenin' my mind. You here?

SAMUEL. I am. The word spoken about town is you ran north…

HARRIET. I intend that be the word, an' I need your help…

SAMUEL. I bought your children. They are with your Grandmother…

HARRIET. Thank you…for purchasing, *(beat) my* children. I am in need of a favor.

SAMUEL. Knowing you are here places me in the precarious position of harboring a fugitive… I do not feel at all comfortable.

HARRIET. Yes. I too am uncomfortable. I must request a favor. I beg that you help me, perhaps in remembrance of pleasant times we have spent together…

SAMUEL. I am here, you may as well make the request.

HARRIET. I have written several letters, I have addressed them from myself to my former Master,

SAMUEL. Legally you are still…

HARRIET. Of course…my Master… I only ask that you take these letters on your travels north and from time to time mail them to Master Norcom as though they are from me.

SAMUEL. I have always admired your cleverness…

HARRIET. I think you have, on occasion, been amused by my cleverness…

SAMUEL. I shall do this…

HARRIET. Thank you.

SAMUEL. Take care of yourself Harriet.

(SAMUEL exits.)

HARRIET. *(muttering to herself)* Take care of yourself Harriet. Harriet you take care of yourself. Yes Master… I be sure do that…be sure to "take care of myself" because that is what I have always done. I "take care of myself." An' the voices don' stop…

(HARRIET exits to hiding space.)

MARY. Once I cleanin' up de missus room. I sebben. She nine. She come in an' say, "Watchu doin'?" An' I say, cleanin your room an' she say, "Why?" an' I say, "'Cause my mama ask me to" an she say, "Uh uh you cleanin' my room 'cause you blong to me like my toys." An then she say, "Anything I ask you to do you have to do it, 'cause you belong to me." An' truly I din' know what she talkin' 'bout so I say you need to move so's I can finish my work and she slap me, hard, an' den she start to cry, an her mama come in and an she say "Mary won' do like I ask," an' her mama call my mama, make her turn me over her knee, bare my bottom an' beat me wif de hair side a brush 'til I bleed. Dat's de firs' time I got a real whuppin. Still didn' understand what she meant by "I own you." Still don quite understand how someone can say dey own me when dey not God.

> (**HARRIET** *has reappeared in space,* **MARY***'s focus shifts from house to* **HARRIET***.*)

MARY. Harriet, I still here. Harriet?

HARRIET. Mary, I sorry.

> (**MARY***'s light out.* **MASTER NORCOM***'s rises.*)

MASTER NORCOM. I can smell you up there Harriet.

HARRIET. Didn't Tom kill you?

MASTER NORCOM. That was a while ago now. I'm back. And I can smell you.

> (*In the distance we see* **BENNY** *and* **ELLEN** *standing, holding hands, backs to audience. They sing a simple children's song…it is haunting. [It is not necessary that the children we see produce the sound, interesting in fact if it seems otherworldly, but is unmistakably the voice of children.]*)

MASTER NORCOM. I can smell you.

HARRIET. No.

MASTER NORCOM. I most certainly can.

HARRIET. 'Cause you like a dog. 'Cause you like a bloodhound.

MASTER NORCOM. Careful how you speak to me. Even in your mind I can crush you and your little bastard porch monkeys.

HARRIET. No! No! No! In my mind you are nothing but a sad little man. Not even man enough to convince a slave girl to be with you. An' how hard could it be really. Look at me. You own me. I can't even claim my

own fingernails, and you sniff 'round me actin' jealous
and foolish…

> (**MASTER**'s *light goes out* – **HARRIET** *hears the
> children's singing, maybe for the first time.*)

Children? Children!

> (*The children turn, as if searching for the location
> of the voice as the light goes out.*)

(*pause, to audience:*) In the dark there is time to think,
an' remember.

SAMUEL SAWYER, MASTER NORCOM, TOM. You the prettiest
little black thing I ever laid my eyes on.

HARRIET. Tom?

TOM. Harriet.

HARRIET. Samuel?

SAMUEL. I say, you the prettiest little black thing I ever laid
my eyes on.

HARRIET. Why I cain't jes be the prettiest little thing? Why
it got to be a black before it. You tell white gals, dey de
prettiest little white gals?

SAMUEL SAWYER AND MASTER NORCOM. Why not jest take a
compliment as it's given?

HARRIET. Didn' you kill him Tom?

TOM. I did.

> (**MASTER**'s *light goes out.*)

SAMUEL SAWYER. I say, why not just take the compliment.

HARRIET. Why not give a compliment right?

SAMUEL SAWYER. Harriet, some day you will learn to watch
your mouth 'round the people who mean you well.

HARRIET. Tom…

TOM. Harriet?

HARRIET. You let him talk to me this way?

TOM. No dear Harriet… I kill him too if you like…

> (**SAMUEL**'s *lights go out.*)

HARRIET. *(to audience)* When it's too cold, or too hot, or I am especially scared…the voices don' say what I need them to…

TOM. I heard you have two half-breeds.

HARRIET. It's true. You seen them? How they look?

TOM. I hear they ain't the Master's.

HARRIET. It would be better for you if they were?

TOM. Maybe.

HARRIET. I hear things too Tom, an' I hear you settled down with a house girl from your own plantation. You have a liken' for house girls Tom?

TOM. I loved you.

HARRIET. But you didn't come back.

TOM. He took our future and he burned it, and what was I to say to you 'bout that? How was I to explain that I gave myself up for you and it got burned, and there ain't nothing left. That little gal I married don't know me Harriet. She has half a man, and that's all she'll ever have, 'cause that's all that's left. But, for her, half a man is enough. For you, you deservin' of a full man.

HARRIET. You shoulda come…

TOM. You shouldna laid down with a white man.

(Lights up on NORCOM.)

MASTER NORCOM. I can smell you up there Harriet.

(CHILDREN, backs still to audience, appear on a different part of the stage. We hear strands of their music.)

HARRIET. You need to get out my head.

(TOM's light fades.)

Not you!

(TOM's rises, CHILDREN's light begins to fade…)

MASTER NORCOM. I can smell you up there

HARRIET. YOU!

> (**MASTER**'s *light out,* **CHILDREN**'s *song fades slowly through the following. A barely recognizable version of their song plays quietly beneath:*)

HARRIET. Or maybe that's not how it goes. Maybe it goes more like this, yes, this is how I make it go...

TOM. You all right up in that tight space?

HARRIET. No Tom, it hurts.

TOM. I'm sorry. I truly wish I could ease your pain.

HARRIET. Thank you.

TOM. Saw your babies playing in the yard. They pretty. Look like they mama.

HARRIET. Thank you Tom.

TOM. I miss you Harriet.

HARRIET. I miss you Tom, always will.

TOM. When we escape to the north together...

HARRIET. And that's as far as I can... So, mostly, I think and dream of my children.

> (*Light rises on previous tableau of children, further downstage, we hear faintly their song.*)

Grandma told me to try to protect my heart, to love my children only as much as is necessary, but no more. I know she knows this is impossible. I make a sharp tool with the handle of my slop bucket and bore a little hole in the roof here. I can look out and see them in the yard. First they babies, tied round they middles with string to the clothesline so they not wander far. I see my boy eat dirt, an' I cain't say nothin'. I see my baby girl poke my boy in the eye an he cry, an she laugh. I see dem later, bigger, make figures on the ground with dirt. I want to help them make letters. I see Granma scoop them up an take them in to dinner. I see puffs of hair turn into long braids with ribbon... I see them growing, strong and happy and healthy.

> (*Light abruptly goes out on children.*)

Seven years I watch them grow an' can't touch them.

(We hear the children's voices, but don't see them through the following.)

GIRL. Mama. I knowed you come back.

HARRIET. You *knew* I'd come back.

GIRL. Das what I said. I knowed you come back. And here you is.

HARRIET. Yes. Here I is.

BOY. You bring us presents?

HARRIET. Yes baby boy. Sure did.

BOY. You bring candy?

HARRIET. All the candy you want forever.

GIRL. We don't want candy, we jes want you to stay.

HARRIET. Always. I always be right here. Right here where you can run to when you need me. An' I protect you, an' I keep you safe, an' I keep you warm. An' you only have to answer to me.

BOY. I thought we only have to answer to God.

HARRIET. You only have to answer to God and me.

GIRL. I love you Mama.

HARRIET. I love you too baby. *(to **BOY**)* What about you?

BOY. I cain't say that. Don' wan' sound like a girl. But you is a good mama.

HARRIET. I am a good mama.

BOY. Granny say it not good to flatter yourself.

HARRIET. An' that's as far as I can imagine it...or I will scream. Or die.

*(**GRANDMA** enters. She sets down a basket of food and a slop jar.)*

GRANDMA. You won't die.

HARRIET. Grandma? That you? You real?

GRANDMA. Who else it be? How I not be real? An, don' be talkin' bout dyin'.

HARRIET. All these years. Maybe death be better.

GRANDMA. You choose death, the Master wins. You decided this where you need to be… Come down here, Granny need to talk to your face.

HARRIET. It's near day Granny, you think it safe?

GRANDMA. None of this never was safe… Come down here, I'll check your head for lice while we talk.

*(While **HARRIET** leaves her space, **GRANDMA** speaks:)*

Mary missin' you. Come over here talkin' bout how she think even the Missus wish you was there 'cause things at the house so slow an' boring now. Says she take care of the chilluns in the big house now an' they be askin' after you all the time.

*(**HARRIET** has emerged and settles, painfully, on the floor by **GRANDMA**. **GRANDMA** begins parting and examining the hair.)*

HARRIET. I been up there a long time Grandma.

GRANDMA. Too long baby. You got another letter for me to give Massa Samuel?

HARRIET. Yes. I even wrote in it fo Massa Norcom to tell you It's OK.

GRANDMA. You sure this all part of your plan an' not just pride.

HARRIET. It true, I'm prideful of outsmarting Massa Norcom, but also, it seem like a good way to go 'bout it. Let me read you the letter: "Dear Master Norcom, I surely hope God and you and de Missus can forgive me. I ran 'cause my bein' there ain't helpin' the fambly. I's sorry I had dem babies outta wedlock an' I ain't a good example to set for the chilluns…" But this the part, I like this part best… I write… "I do hope your investment in bounty hunters does not drain your family's resources. Might I suggest you donate those funds to the church coffers, or even allow Mistress Norcom a new dress, as I will not be found."

GRANDMA. I hate to see you anger him so…

HARRIET. *(amused)* Do you really Granny?

GRANDMA. *(laughing)* ...No... It makes me quite proud. *(beat)* It does seem there's more Massa Sam could do to make it easier for you.

HARRIET. You knew he wouldn't. *(beat)* Grandma, I ain't fifteen no more. I did think he was special then. Really I did. He was kind, and seem like he the only man I was gone be with an' not feel like I break into pieces. Think I even made myself call it love. Probly deep inside I didn't never really think he was gone carry me off on a horse an make me the first niggra mistress of a plantation. Didn' wanna be first negro mistress. I jes needed a place to rest my head and put my heart and put my hopes, an' he there, an he not the Doctor, an' I cain't have Tom, an I think, God forgive me, I would do it again.

GRANDMA. Hush girl, you ain't got to 'splain... *(beat)* It's been too long. I think even Mary get suspicious, she come by an all the time I be comin' from the shed, yesterday she even say "Seem like you go out there more'n you used to. Seem like I may be not the only one will notice that."

HARRIET. That mighty clever for Mary.

GRANDMA. I thought so too. *(long beat)* I worked out passage for you on a ship what sails north. Cap'n a good white man, always liked your Granny, an do us this favor for a small fortune. He hide you *with* the cargo, an once you out to sea, you darken your skin an' pose as his servant girl...you dock somewhere near New York an' we got the underground to hide you an' direct you to a safe house in Boston.

HARRIET. I won' see my babies again.

GRANDMA. They ain't babies no more. An' the way you see them now makin' you feel better? You die up here, or lose your senses, they still won' have a mama...an' God forbid you found out an' we all put in jail or worse.

HARRIET. They good kids ain't they?

GRANDMA. Yes.

HARRIET. They gone be good people?

GRANDMA. Yes.

HARRIET. They gone be safe an' happy an' healthy?

GRANDMA. Might be.

HARRIET. You think one day they be free.

GRANDMA. They free now.

HARRIET. Not long as Massa Sam got papers on them. He marry the wrong kind or get thrown from a horse an' they be on the block tomorrow...

GRANDMA. I almost got the money to buy them outright. They gone be alright.

HARRIET. No such thing as alright in this place.

GRANDMA. You been talkin' to God since you been up here?

HARRIET. I pray. Sometime I think he even listen ...But sometime I think I don't know who I'm talkin' to.

GRANDMA. You jes know this. People long 'fore you, people now, people live years after you be lost an' sufferin' an it don't mean cain't find a private peace in the middle of it. *(beat)* Oh Lord, I been gone too long. You get yourself ready.

HARRIET. Yes ma'am.

> (**GRANDMA** *exits.* **ENSEMBLE** *hums a lullaby. We see the children climb into hiding space with* **HARRIET**. *They cuddle in. They are, in that moment, for that time, re-united, the lighting indicates night turning into day.* **HARRIET** *whispers over the sleeping children to the audience.)*

Grandma let me have a goodbye with the children, being careful not to tell them where I was going. It seems Benny had known for the last three years. His little ears heard me sneeze while playing in the yard with a friend. My angel kept it to himself, away from his sister, an' Grandma, steering friends to a different part of the yard whenever they played. It is sad and miraculous, the way slavery makes men of our boys and women of our girls in the most surprising ways.

> (**HARRIET** *untangles herself from the sleeping children, giving each a last kiss and covering them with the blankets. The* **ENSEMBLE** *emerge from the back and take up the hymn. Eventually it will morph into an uplifting song of freedom.*)

I have always wanted to think that things happen for a reason. It comforts me to think that maybe horrible things happen so that they will never happen again. But no, that is too easy. I think horrible things happen because they do. But I do believe that we find a way. That we are human, and so we must find a way. And it gets better until it gets worse, and it gets better again and sometimes a little worse, and maybe later, better even than that. My hiding place was small, but in it, my soul was able to soar. In it, even when my body hurt more than I have the words to describe, I was more free than any bill of sale would ever make me. I did find my way North. Eventually, once grown, my children even made their way to me... I found a life rich with the joys and sorrows of, a life. But it was above Grandmother's shed, in the cold and the dark, in the heat and the solitude, that I found my voice...so that my voice might find its way into the world... In that tight, dark place my mind grew, my heart expanded and with a pen and scraps of paper I was able to stretch my arms out...

> (**ENSEMBLE** *members have gathered around her and have begun singing a rousing, hopeful spiritual. It is not a celebration...it is an affirmation of life.* **HARRIET** *stands still. She is not triumphant, there is not happiness, there is rather the conviction of one who will survive...the satisfaction of one who will tell her story...the need to know that she has been heard. She walks upstage into the deep blue sky of the future.*)

(*Lights fade on all.*)

End of Play

www.ingramcontent.com/pod-product-compliance
Lightning Source LLC
Chambersburg PA
CBHW072021290426
44109CB00018B/2302